THE DREAMHOUSE

PHOENIX **POETS**

A SERIES EDITED BY ALAN SHAPIRO

The Dreamhouse

TOM SLEIGH

THE UNIVERSITY OF CHICAGO PRESS
Chicago and London

Among Tom Sleigh's many honors are the 1999
Shelley Award of the Poetry Society of America,
grants from the National Endowment for the Arts
and the Guggenheim Foundation, and the Lila
Wallace–Reader's Digest Fund's Individual
Writer's Award. He teaches at Dartmouth College.

The University of Chicago Press, Chicago 60637
The University of Chicago Press, Ltd., London
© 1999 by The University of Chicago
All rights reserved. Published 1999

08 07 06 05 04 03 02 01 00 99   1 2 3 4 5

ISBN 0-226-75048-5 (cloth)
       0-226-75049-3 (paper)

Library of Congress Cataloging-in-Publication Data

Sleigh, Tom.
        The dreamhouse / Tom Sleigh.
            p. cm. — (Phoenix poets)
        ISBN 0-226-75048-5 (cloth : alk. paper)
        ISBN 0-226-75049-3 (paper: alk. paper)
        I. Title. II. Series.
    PS3569.L36D74 1999   98-43615
    811'.54—dc21   CIP

♾ The paper used in this publication meets the
minimum requirements of the American National
Standard for Information Sciences—Permanence
of Paper for Printed Library Materials,
ANSI Z39.48-1992.

for Ellen

Contents

III

IV

Acknowledgments

Grateful acknowledgment is made to the following magazines in which many of these poems first appeared:

Agni: "To the Sun"
Alaska Quarterly: "Under the Pines"
Bomb: "Raft," "Speech for Myself as a Ghost"
Boston Book Review: "Bond," "The Cry," "Flesh," "The Wreck"
Boston Phoenix: "The Dreamhouse," "The Door"
Boston Review: "After Midnight"
Greensboro Review: "The Island"
Harvard Review: "Purity Supreme"
Ploughshares: "A Visit"
Poetry: "The Harbor"
Provincetown Arts: "The Field"
Raritan: "Fragment," "Heracles"
Slate: "Augusto Jandolo: On Excavating an Etruscan Tomb," "Demon,"
    "Prayer," "The Ticket" ©1998 Microsoft Corporation
TriQuarterly: "The Fight," "The Grid," "Transfusion"
Yale Review: "The Hammock," "Scattering"

I would also like to thank the Lila Wallace–Reader's Digest Fund for an Individual Writer's Award, 1992–95.

Prayer

God of flesh, god of pleasure,
give us leisure while we're still strong—

                              defend us

from the whirlwind that blights
ash leaves with lesions,

                          that makes the black cypress shake

like the junkie I saw begging on the corner.

Calm the undertow of the sea,
make the world

                    go slow as shadows

shifting as the sun shifts
in the garden of Persephone.

We kneel at the foot of oblivion's alp,
waiting for the snow to melt,

                       for the stream

fretted with ice
to crack like a pistol shot,

                  shatter

and flow
as we splash out wine staining the tablecloth.

Keep hidden from us what tomorrow holds—

let's go looking while we can, while the Zone
or the Block or Wareham Street
lures us down onto our knees at night,
                              through parks

and dunes, the Gladiator's Gym
and the Brass Rail . . .

Oh god of flesh, god of pleasure,

keep us in the dark
                    one moment more—

touching hands, lips grazing
lips, flesh
moving into flesh

. . . as the sun goes down
to orgy in the snow
                        on Soracte's slopes
shadowy as bodies giving
                              themselves away.

                    after Horace

The Dreamhouse

Does it move inside him, that trembling of the earth?
Or is it his spirit failing him, teetering and wobbling,
Its gyroscopic spin slowing to a swoon?

And when he mumbles of seven falls descending one into the next,
Is he the one stumbling up the spray-slick wooden steps,
Or is he himself the slowly diffusing spray?

That permeable ocean between him and his death
Overflows the window and lifts him above the waves,
His drenched sheets and his hands limp in his lap

Poised eternally, a bubble about to break . . .
And then the air thickens, weighing down his flesh,
The earth's trembling now too ghostly for him to feel,

The seven falls mere water pouring pool to pool,
His still body afloat in the ether of morphine
Expunged by the glare flooding across the pane . . .

His being, like absence new-minted in the clouds,
Scatters in gusts and squalls. Sheets stripped, his vacant bed
Hovers in the room while moonlight, sunlight

Scrub the walls clean—his closets now emptied,
His clothes dispersed, his face, his eyes doing
A slow dissolve in memory's salt baths

Even as he takes up residence, the dreamhouse
A void all glass and air: one table, one chair,
And sweeping wall to wall to wall sunlight everywhere.

The Cry

Whose body is it anyway, shouts a voice in the street
Before subsiding back into traffic's thrum, *whose body, whose body*
Echoing in my mind as I walk down the Avenue:

Whose body but death's, says the funeral parlor on the corner,
Lilies' shadows looming against the clean cliff of the wall.
The echoes of that cry worm into our muscles, organs, veins,

Even the self-reflexive shimmer of being we call "soul"—it makes us sick,
It opens us the way an ox, sliced open by Rembrandt's eye,
Reveals white fat and bone glimmering through plaited muscle.

Whose body is it? asked Leonardo sketching from his corpses
According to Vitruvius' principles, "De Architectura"
In ten volumes: the body's spread-eagled frailty

Grown heroic in that grid of circle embracing circle
As if the body were a cathedral, vault, cupola, spire . . .
Opening the door, *whose body* asks the wall in my room

Where this morning all morning I sat watching a stain
Bleed through immaculate, snowy bandages of plaster:
First a shadowy profile, like the Souillac Isaiah, then marked out

By that stain, his all-seeing eye that burns through the present
To where bodies finally dwell, both the saved, the damned—
And even there I hear it, under the curses and the praise,

Under the torments of flesh that the prophet
Renders with such relish, his woeful, vatic rant
About righteousness and death unable

To drown out that last vestige of who we were
Before our transfiguration: *We will all be changed
But not all of us will be saved*—so that as we put on

Our eternal incorruption or finally sink down
Into damnation's putrefaction, the worm gnawing in eternally
Or which we witness from on high is still unable

To sever the ghostly substance of that cry
Which vibrates beyond heaven's or hell's flimsy bounds,
Replenishing forever on its own echoes.

After Midnight

After midnight in the summer heat,
the black river of the road flowing out and out,
windows rolled down, tires buoyant as water,

the car floats through the night gone still forever
around the hospital on the hill,
the neon of the ER turning the waiting eyes to glass.

Mist rises from the river,
the moon nowhere in sight,
only thick-leaved trees sweeping the cool black.

Secret in her power, like a sunroof
sliding open to the air, Athena touches you
and makes you, to yourself, younger, stronger

—vital as the river where rats
along the bank breed in the sweet grass
infusing the heavy air,

the radio tower
above the quiet city beaming
from its lone eye a voice sobsinging,

"Spring can really hang you up the most" . . . disenchanted
siren who sings you back into yourself
warily hoarding the charmed strength

of your middle age, your eyes not on the stars
but on a shadow under the trees
like Cyclops in his cave

praying to Poseidon to deliver you
to destruction even as you boast, "My name
is No Man, No Man is my famous name—"

the car hurtling weightless through the open night.

Heracles

Strongman. Father. Provider. Savior.
Killer. Madman who suffered his own strength.
Who he is;
> what he stands for;
>> the riddle
he poses to himself.
> He killed the Nemean lion,
he wrested the world from the old powers
of chimera and monster.
>> Divided mind,
mortal and divine. Perpetual actor
acting out his labors for Eurystheus.
Hated by Hera:
> she guided the serpents
to the shield that cradled him, but he woke
and strangled them in his baby's fists . . .
His mortal nature whispers to his father:
"Why am I like this? Make me something else—
more like an ordinary man."
>> But his divine half
answers:
> "Feel the surge breaking in your brain?
That's the shoal where you've run aground.
Dare to be like others, and the god
in you will rise and drag you down."

2

The abyss
solicits him up to its edge
where he waits
as if waiting at an all-night gas station,
the timeclock ticking in the storage corridor.

The abyss smokes
like a volcano's rim
sulfured by rage, chaos, pain—

it makes him forget
all about the hour
when he dug the channel
to redirect the river
through the shitdeep stable
and washed it clean.

Immeasurable depth.

He balances above it
as if he stood on a cliff
that crumbles into
air unbreathably
subzero and miles long clear.

3

Hair and beard glozed and curled.
He holds the apples from the edge of the world.
The lion's jaws open round his head
serve as his hood.

The paws dangle
over his almost female
nipples, the skin from the legs
tied in a knot. His club is studded; his pectorals'

definition are an aphrodisiac.
In his presence you feel something godlike
thickening the air
as if he moved and breathed in his own special atmosphere.

Everyone knows of his trip to Hell
when he taught Hades' watchdog to wag its tail,
filthy, barking, triple-mouthed monster.
His whole demeanor

as he stands in his carnal, body-builder's
splendor denies that he's conscious
of his effect on others—prodigious
cocksman who watches

his reflection
smooth and harden
to cool marble, his empty-eyed
pupils almost sad.

4

The labors
no one bothered
to record.

His fear and despair
in nerveless motels
while he waited
to face down
whatever monster
he must kill.

Ecstasy. Self-disgust.
Then hours of TV
flickering against
drawn blinds.

The way he nocks
his arrows and murders
in a frenzy
when Madness
in her black chariot
drives straight
into his heart.

His interminable death,
worse than cancer,
his blood infected
by the poison
of Hydra
whom he slew.

The pyre he
built himself
to consume
his mortal flesh
while his divine half
registers each flicker
of the flame.

His loneliness
and awkwardness
in trying to explain
his suspicion
that his pain
is myth,
mere myth.

His knowledge
that his Father
can make him,
when He chooses,
a god.

Ask him who he is
and he'll exclaim:
"Heracles—'Hera's
glory'—she,
who hates me
most of all."

5

"I murdered my wife and children.
Can't you keep me hidden from the sun?"

                              "You're human.
Nothing human can stain what is divine."

"Steer clear of me. Don't touch me. Run from
My infection."

            "When I was in pain, you towed
Me to safety. Now put your hand on my shoulder.
I'll steady you. I'm your friend."

                        "I can't get up.
My legs are like stone."

                  "Necessity
Is a hammer that breaks even the strong."

"I wish I were stone. Blank as stone.
Past grief."

            "That's enough. Take my hand."

"Be careful. I'll stain more than your clothes
With blood."

            "Go on. Stain them. My love for you
Will protect me from infection."

"Did I do all this? My sons? My wife?"

"I only know this: everything you had
Is changed to grief."

                    "Where did I go mad?
Where did my soul betray me?"

                        "There.
By the altar. As you knelt to wash your hands."

6

Expiation? Yes, there was always expiation.

But the ex-sex offender talking on the radio
to another ex-offender, telling him, "Man, I respect you
for your courage in calling in—"
                                        had also said it was a miracle
he'd been clean for thirteen years.

Now that his crimes were out of bounds, he
was his own labor
fighting off his compulsion like Hydra's hundred heads—

he talked about his crimes as an illness
that twisted you tight like a rag
                                        and wrung you out
and how hard you had to fight
to keep that rag from twisting.

Therapy, he said, had shown him that the children he'd hurt were real.

One caller called in:
                        "For what you've stolen from others,
you ought to be put away for life—you ought to be castrated."

And the other replied:
                        "Castration? You can castrate me.
But what do you do about my tongue and hands?"

7

As he strives to be like others,

for each head that his sword

severs,

do two more heads sprout back?

8

"The way unhealth becomes like health,
or a life gone wrong becomes our life, that was how
it was in my embattled life of myth.

While Eurystheus was free to indulge his whims,
I thought I held myself to another standard;
I envisioned my labors opening into volumes

of gold-trimmed pages, of marble busts
staring down colonnades where sinuous fountains
swooned and swayed in afternoon sunbursts

through clouds of greed and power passing through.
Wasn't I a king too, as good as any?
And yet I was bound to my weakling shadow,

at his beck and call to soil my nature
by cleaning out stables so encrusted in shit
they only came clean in the currents of a river.

At first I believed it was what the gods willed—
so many labors, so many sins atoned—
but I felt myself get hooked each time I killed

some poor slob monster not worth the killing,
higher than the sun on my own adrenalin . . .
—In my enemy I saw mirroring

back to me my lust to be other
for a while, pumped up beyond belief,
beyond justice or right or whatever

alibi my divided nature offered.
What was in my way, I cut down.
And then it was me, me standing there

befuddled in the wake of what I'd done:
My life showing clear as one incredible error.
The Gorgon in my eyes turning me to stone."

9

What more can he say
to excuse himself
for having less patience
than he should?

The weakling inside the strongman knew
what the strongman's
limitations were—
a readiness to see in others' eyes

his own good opinion of himself
mirrored back indulgently
whenever he committed
some indiscretion borne of selfishness:

wasn't getting away with it
tantamount to admitting,
"Yes, yes, for you the rules
are suspended—"

his self-absolving leniency
that clubbed down objections
in the court of his vanity
where love for others—

especially one other—
meant treating that person
like a twin.
But more than a twin,

a shadow self to whom
all one's self-seeking
was devoted . . .
For all his malignant cupidity,

when he realized what
he'd killed by not reckoning
with the consequence
of his own worst desire, he felt

so seared by fires of
shame that he barely noticed
his own funeral pyre's flames
singeing his mortal half

from the immortal
—and as his divinity wrestled
to get free, he found himself
staring up into a face

whose eyes pitied him for the fire
he burned in
but whose gaze already roved
beyond the flames.

10

Aren't those gods, gods feasting?
Or is it an illusion?
He asks himself this question,
stalled between sleep and waking.

Wine-glimmer on a caterer's table.
Echoes in the vaulted hall
wild in his ear.
No blood anywhere,

nothing like that in
the bronzed faces ringing him
to remind him of the place
from which he came.

Now he is stirring.
What will he see
when he finally wakes?
All the old errors, mistakes

burned clear? His soul
turning round and round
like an animal sniffing out
the sour smell of exile?

Libations in fluted glasses . . .
Pupils unflecked by blood . . .
Marble busts . . . marbled walls . . .
His statue's battered scowl.

11

After the flames had burned all there was to burn,
the mortal part risen into smoke while the immortal looked on,
he entered the dead's dark city for the second time.
Here, substance no longer feared the insubstantial,
"mist" and "flesh" became the shadow rhyme.
His labors were done. Who he was was annulled
in this spectral communion of weak and strong.
The blood and flies and smoke that stung his memory
faded like a bruise into unmarked skin, the nightlong
vigils he'd practiced as a child, trying to allay
his fear of monsters he would quell when he grew up,
the only discipline he needed now to save
himself from the carnage of dreams. Now he could slip
away from the too bright sun that lit the no-quarter duels
which were his destined fame . . . He feels himself narrow, he can feel
a hand stronger than his that mingles love and terror
seize him and sight down his length as if he were an arrow,
that power bending like a bow and the bowstring strung
so that he shivers anticipating the song it will sing
when the hand draws back, fits him to the string and the bow's curved will.
In the world above, his labors will decorate vases, coins, a golden shield,
but here there is nothing left for him to do, nothing left to fulfill
but what the feathered shaft will set in motion. Before him the underworld
shrinks to an arrow's tip, behind him his past bleeds into a vapor trail
until he is nothing but the momentum he feels gathering
as the bow bends and the tensing fingers curl.

Fragment

. . . and round the shield's rim ran the stream of Ocean
Looking in full flood and lapping at each scene
Hephaestos fashioned there, the great shield
Zeus ordained for Heracles, his son, to hold
Back death in battle.
                                And on it were swans,
Some with wings spread wide darkening the heavens
As they sang, while others swam on the waters far below
And swerving fish bolted shadow to shadow.

Augusto Jandolo: On Excavating an Etruscan Tomb

"When we lit our torches
My eyes went blind in the cave's
Cool dark—

        the damp rock rough against my palms,
I remember how we strained to lift

                the great stone lid: slowly
It rose, stood on end . . . then fell
Heavily aside, crashing down

            in the smoky,
Turbulent light
So that just for an instant I saw—
It wasn't a skeleton I saw;

          not bones,
But a body, the arms and legs stiffly outstretched—
A young warrior's flesh still dressed
In armor, with his helmet, spear, shield, and greaves
As though he'd just been laid in the grave:

For just that moment
Inside the sarcophagus I saw the dead live—

                                    but then, beneath
The sea-change of our torches,
At the first touch of air, the warrior
Who'd lain there, his body inviolable
For centuries, dissolved—

                  dissolved, as we looked on,
Into dust . . .
                  his helmet rolling right, his round shield sagging
Into the void beneath his breastplate, the greaves
Collapsing as his thighs gave way . . .

                                    But in the aura
Round our torches a golden powder
Rose up in the glow and seemed to hover."

II

Demon

Cars stalled, the light gone
hazy under leafless sycamores—
                              nature's
diction, as casual as you asking
for a last glass of water, whispers in my ear
words cotton-mouthed and sere as sloughing bark
littering the roadway,
                      rush hour traffic
halting, faltering like my hand
the day I signed away your flesh
to the crematory fire . . .

Now, the white lines' dot and dash
makes my hand less steady on the wheel,
the stoplight glimmers a shade too red—
the faith I've never felt in the day to day
haunts me like some imp-winged demon
in a Bosch painting, its infantile, red-bawling face
staring accusingly into my eyes
as if it dared to fly beyond the gilt frame,
hectoring, hovering, sluggish wings buzzing
like the winter-hatched fly stumbling
spastic against the dashboard dials,
its frail internal compass somehow gone haywire
overridden by spurts and shocks.

Beneath the roadside sycamores,
as if a newsreel unspooled in my head,
I see a squirrel, gaunt, great-eyed
as a prisoner half-starved, its face dissolving
into the demon's face

                  . . . so like my father's face
quizzical, half-angry, pinched by death;
and then, at the end, grown grave, calm . . .

                                     mendicant

as a fly, its legs bent as if to pray,
the great swiveling head a friar's
black hood, Mephistophilis disguised

—*Why, this is hell, nor am I out of it* . . .

Among the quivering needles the fly
smashes, its imp-wings
glimmering in the cooling light, its demon eyes
shattered into broken mirrors
replicating *ad infinitum* car car car car
tree tree tree . . . now it lands on the steering wheel
and faces me:
                  What do I look like
in the eyes of a fly?
                      Shattered into nose lips eyes
do my jittering faces swarm like harbingers of
the demon in my own last act
who takes off his hood and shows me my signature
signed in blood . . . ?
                      but it's you, isn't it?,
you staring out from those bulging eyes
asking frankly for my sympathy, yet timid,
apologetic, only doing your job—
my familiar flying through rising fumes
to drag me from the car.

The Island

After our last week together
In that seaside condominium
I thought that you had left me forever—
But now you come to me, come

Holding out the drug I swore to overdose
You on had you lasted one more day . . .
Then Cyclops, Scylla and Charybdis,
Bereft of their old enemy,

Implore me to end their misery—
But I can't—my hand is too unsteady,
You shake your head at them and me,
Merciless in your mercy . . .

Now, more and more you pull away,
Entering the absence my childhood
Taught me became a father—yet how thoughtlessly
We used to travel to the world of the dead

And back again, the shunt in your arm
Cycling your blood through the clear tubing
—So red, so live, so richly warm
Yet fabulous as the Sirens singing,

Their voices mingling with the other patients'
Voices, the room like an island
Of living and dying, of sense
And senselessness . . . As in a dream I stand

Next to you, watching your blood
Voyage beyond your veins, my hand
Resting lightly on your bony shoulder blade:
And know that when I turn the island

Will dissolve to inchoate
Shimmerings of ocean and blinding sun,
Your footstep so light not a grain
Of sand shifts beneath its weight.

Under the Pines

Down the nave of twisted pines
like green flame out of dust
you flare quick as gasoline
above the pigeons flocking

to the patio: the branches
behind you sprout
from your shoulders, green wings
of the hummingbird

outflanking that processional,
your zigzag flight mocking
the straight lines of the garden,
your whirring wings

slashing the gauze net of your name.
Your feathers' breath
smokes along my cheek
until the air between us kindles

to crematory flame, your black quill's
syringe plunged
in narcotic honeysuckle
scattering petals

overblown, the unyielding
brightness of your eyes
oblivious to mine . . . Now, only in dreams
do you walk with me again,

my name familiar on your tongue
as these pines you planted . . .
My new-fledged silent one,
does any trace of me still linger

in that birdseye sidelong stare
coolly unblinking
as if to lure me closer,
my hands closing round

your clean veer
and hover?—then swerving
off too quick
to follow after.

Scattering

Not buried by the highways or in the ruined temples
but in the anonymous margins between fields:
A steel box of ashes, the ashes slick and greasy on my palm.

Rainwater glistening in the furrows, underfoot a sea of mud.
Battered wreaths of rusted wire. Sunlight hazes
the still air, puddles of mirage brim and overflow.

Field after field runs to the horizon while ashes fade
into heatwaves the way a swimmer fades
into a slick of glare. The Persians lie north and south,

the Megarians and Phoenicians place their heads to the east,
the Athenians toward the west, which the Christians
still retain. I turn to the ghost beside me and feel

that slight mass fusing with my heaviness,
not lightening my flesh but making each step harder.
Cypress, fir, yew, the earth's pyre burning sweet fuel

perpetually verdant, the soul's harmonic nature
chiming with the spheres. Stubbornly hoping,
protected by happy fraud against excessive lamentation,

the ancients believe deep sorrows disturb their ghosts
—but all is vanity, feeding the wind and folly,
Nimrod lost in Orion, Osiris in the Dog-star . . .

The invisible sun within us. Our fathers find
their graves in our short memories, and sadly tell us
how we may be buried in our survivors.

And though Elias prophesies the world may last
but six thousand years, still the grain springs back:
Horizon to horizon the wheat grows even thicker.

III

Bond

Stillness. Abandon. Genius with words.

Your presence. Your absence. The moment
When presence turns into absence, stillness into sound.
Balance of mind shifting to imbalance.
Lover of stillness, absence, presence,
Lover of earth, self, word. Despiser of that love.
Voice of mind pure speaking in the ether, violent voice
Lording it over matter. Matter revenging itself on voice.
Void replete with nullity, a kind of death-not-death
That speaks inside the heart's openness
And can never be forgotten once heard in extremity
That becomes one condition of our day to day.
Your presence that words cast their shadow over
Like a tree in leaf going out of leaf.
Style of your presence which is how I know you
Even in the ashpit of Jehosaphat, your swimmer's stroke
Through waves of fire the same here as there.
Genius of your presence ineluctably yours
Though subject to inertia in which all things come to rest.
Moments of your voice that establish the words
That make up the bond unbreakable between us
That keeps on breaking no matter what we do,
The breaking the bond unbreakable between us.

Presence moving into genius with words moving into abandon, stillness.

Stillness

Slow waking in this stillness so luxurious
No separation between flesh heat and blanket heat,
The hungry eye enchanted by your belts draped across the mirror,

Your yellow silk shirt, red sash, black obi;
Then a tremor in the self deep down,
Self gathering and disadhering from warmth

Diffused through sheets, blankets,
And inexplicably—*why? why?*—a moment
Of inconsolate reproach, regret?

Where are you this early, you're not here in bed
But off in the apartment doing something so silent
Your absence makes your stillness that much more pronounced—

Fueling appetite the way oil fuels flame,
Appetite compounding
Like avalanching vowels we heard one night

In Brooklyn's nasal intonations, wheezing, panting,
The old poet can't catch his breath, he has to sit down,
Minutely trembling by his reading's end, and gulp his pill . . . surviving

Palate cancer, his own renunciation of cigarettes and liquor
That fed, but gnawed at, his gift . . . his need to derange,
Rearrange his senses so ferocious that our bedroom's stillness

Which seemed luxurious, uncompromised pleasure,
Now makes me wonder,
What burrows beneath this stillness?

And what about the time you and I watched the old poet trying
To maneuver his wildly wrecked flesh into a Volkswagen Bug's back seat,
Legs balky with booze, but with a tightrope walker's

Tight-lipped insouciance before the stretching wire;
And following behind, a younger *poète maudit*,
Who nearly passed out during his own reading, staggering back

From the podium but catching himself,
And then, almost miraculous, recovering his poise,
His voice's generous inflections . . . though afterward, his eyes

Glazed over with Scotch and beer—his affect gone flat,
Isolation thick as the ice pack round the crippled hunter
Frozen for millennia in a crevasse.

—The old poet bends to get into the car, rockily wobbling,
Almost pratfalling with that mirthless comedy
Of utter drunkenness, equilibrium shifted from belly

Into brain, an ice pick driven deep
Into *medulla oblongata*;
But he's almost in, he hunkers down behind the door,

The car, squat, so reminding me of Charon's boat,
Vergil's shade exhorting Dante to endure,
That I'm aware of something more,

Some boundary that we cross but can't cross back,
The old poet's voice echoing in that far stillness
Unapproachable, unimpeachable from here.

—What lurks in the stillness between words?
Is it something like syphilis that can slowly drive me mad
Until I go down on hands and knees

To devour my own excrement
While still straining after light chill and clean . . . ?
Or is it only what's there already,

The way wood checks and splits down the grain—
Each hairline fissure in our bedroom's stillness
Threatening to crack open, swallow your voice and mine

Until all that's left to us is stillness . . . ?
Fear of my own cravings, fear that we pay
For every leaf in our laurels

Made the old poet in his tabloid fame
Like some starkly lit actor in a Mystery play devolving
About age and death and intoxicating appetite,

Not booze as such but a craving that undermines,
That reaches from the ooze to take us
By the ankles, wrestling us down . . .

And now the *maudit* approaches the car door
Weaving—but not *maudit*, just a man drinking, drinking . . . who,
A friend told me, would cry out in the movies as if the scenes

Were all too present, the gigantomachia
Before him the scale that I imagine
His appetites to be at home in, Andromache

And mad Heracles like aunt and uncle
In his private, hallucinatory world
Of the hyper-real . . .

First his head, seat of words, buzzing hive
Of language ducks from sight, then his bowed back,
Sad khakis tight across his ass, one leg, the other,

Scuffed shoe that hovers wavering off the ground
But not yet in the car . . .
—My last sight of him, I realize now,

Before his obituary (wire-photo face
Grainy as through a sandstorm) detailing
His fall from grace on a morals charge,

Then his willful slip or leap from a building,
Joining Berryman, Crane, Empedocles . . .
Now they're both squeezed in, invisible behind dark glass

Until the Bug's lights flash on and I see them
Silhouetted in the back seat not talking, and as I
Try to make sense of them and my own crude gawking,

(Are they cautionary, exemplary, happy, in despair?)
The *maudit* in slow motion turns his face to the window,
A laugh like a grimace twisting his fleshy mouth—

His Janus mask so comprehensive of his fate
And which he himself seems wholly unaware of
That its plaster-eyed, unreadable stare

Rivets our bedroom's stillness in which you have vanished,
Stillness that blows and drifts, seeping through each second,
Which preserves, restrains, and destroys—

Articulate stillness that as I call to you,
Trying to ward it off, *Hey, where are you, I need you, come here,*
Keeps sifting grain by grain into my mouth.

Token

Pitted and hollowed out,
a miniature moon,
this chunk of magma spawned
in earth's boiling core

then spewed into
the freezing upper air
glistens with flecks
of amethyst and iron—

mineral proof
of what each day
teaches us the hard way
in the other's baffled stare

unfathomable as
Empedocles who leaped
into the smoking cone
to prove his flesh divine

while our own nerves shying
from that blistering flame
learn that love and discord
discord and love build up

earth air water fire
then casually tear them down:
Lava seethes toward
olive groves shivering

in the night, fields
and houses bulldozed
by the flow's
incandescent weight . . .

Burning black in late
October sun, on the freshly
painted sill this stone
brings the heart to heel,

each crystal glinting
with that alluring heat
which coaxes us forward
even as we hesitate:

Coolly we calculate,
then glide to the attack,
the whole house smoldering
with words we can't take back—

Faces streaked with dust
and ash, we stumble
in the other's path,
then peer up into jets

of fountaining fire,
the gods' voices rumbling
in the fuming smother
promising us what—

to lift us if we leap?
Gases swooning from
rocky flues and fissures,
each touch extinguishing

the touch before,
we climb the burnt-out slope
to the crater's
molten lip.

The Hammock

Your hand pushes me away
so that I float into the night,
then swing back, back from the nebulae
to our drifting conversation.

Among the race of star demons
what I saw out there—
golden chains, the spindle, sirens
chanting the music of the spheres—

blurs and streaks across star-flung
distances the chain-link fences
can't fence out. Between
your hand and the hammock's

slow rocking the Void
expands, twisting threads
tautening, slackening, stretched
almost to breaking:

Do you feel that wobble
of earth's axis, space
whirling past the ice-capped pole?
The pines like judges stare down at us:

What should we recant, here,
tonight, as if we'd only just begun:
Off-center already, losing
equilibrium? The world-soul moving

through the strung-out stars moves
in threads that creak and moan,
breathes between your mouth and mine.
Pushing me away, you bring

me home, your attraction drawing
down the alchemical sign:
*Love draws the soul
the way a magnet draws iron.*

The Meadow

Across the road from where we nap
under a dead elm dazzles the meadow
where the partisans strung the traitors up,

the meadow which their dangling shadows stain.
Belly up in vines a blasted tank
rusts flake by flake to lichened scrap iron

while horseflies harangue
the rippling green, July
a limbo of quavering yellow . . .

We wake to cattle lowing at dawn,
grass overgrowing summer—so like us
in love each hour with the noonday sun

that neither toils nor spins, its brightness
hovering, blinding us . . .
What would the dead say if they could see us,

lounging, talking, peering through brambles
at cemetery photographs sunk beneath
the undertow of milkweed shadows,

death dates smoothing back into the stone?
I think of Goya's demon, old man flesh
hanging from his bones, long teeth bared in

an ass's grin as he scrawls on a schoolboy's
slate, *What more can be done? Nothing* . . .
while behind him a noose etched clean as

the moon rises through the inkblot
spiraling back into the hanged man's mouth
as if blackness poured from his throat:

"When will you tire of us bogeymen,
caricatures of your father's war,
our crimes half-forgotten, unforgiven?

All future blotted out when they hauled us
from our beds, our minds went dead
to everything but fear: Nightshirts

soaked in snowlight's pall, we hunched in mud, each step
loud, too loud beside the farmhouse wall,
the seconds teetering till we drop . . .

What our betrayals were we know
with a knowledge intimate beyond revenge,
history the needle's eye you can't squeeze through.

The partisans cut us down, heaped us
in a mass grave our relatives dug up: Yes,
there were tears—even for us . . .

Now, like aliens from space on your TV shows,
we ravel into mist, surrounding
you the moment your eyes close . . .

Our pupils search out yours from behind
the mirror with your fathers' stares,
fathers and sons melding in one mind—

but who are you to call us traitors, an outsider
judging through the smoke-haze of home:
Each blow exact, our own neighbors

beat us till the blood ran, beat us black
and blue . . . Even now, would they dare take us back,
older, wiser, necks broken by the yoke?

Moving in time as to a dance we buzz
and swarm across the meadow, dissolving
and glinting like fireflies in the hedge,

blown like milkweed in the moon's wall eye.
But under your lids, you see us locked in cold,
shattered wheatstraw flecked in ice:

Chill as the night air on your sunburned neck
our eyes like X rays pierce the frost,
stalking every step the living take."

The Harp

Stopped at a light halfway to the terminal,
I felt you adrift in the distance between
The visible and the invisible:
Your father in your face, my father in mine,

They both seemed present in the rearview mirror,
Their breath bated, refusing us a sign:
When I glanced, I saw only the car
Behind, not even their shadows for consolation,

No Orpheus like a father leading them back home . . .
—But then through the half-blinding shimmer
Of the windshield that began to swim
And race like the surface of a river

We saw the harp canted in a nearby window,
A gilded half-heart that palpitated in
The sun, then receded into shadow,
Bobbing, light-dripping like an ocean fan

Or a seahorse buffeted by bubbles
Swirling from the bottom of an aquarium.
The distance between my hand and the wheel
Grew to the distance between the harp and the sun,

Taut strings humming in the engine's overtones:
I could almost hear their breathing cradled
In your lungs and mine, their words light as atoms
Above the traffic fumes, those cool, paternal

Syllables, estranging and estranged, telling us to go on—
But the harp keeps us there, hovering, spellbound
By the orphaned voices of its tune,
All eyes and ears, nothing before or behind.

The Outcast

Looking up from his drink
he blinks an eye and ten years
skein by, his longed-for wife
and infant son

etched into his brain
by the acid of his
self-scorn . . . Now he studies
in the tabletop

his scabbed face dirty
as a derelict's, beard
tangled on his tanned chest,
fingers long and delicate;

the terrace rolling
like a sinking ship,
he tests his nerve
for the voyage home:

His eyes dredge
the whirlpooling deep,
nape prickling
as the monster strikes—

its swarming heads
are too fast for him,
they gobble him up
the way the darkening blue

swallows the divers
sinking down and down
to where the wrecks
break up on the reef . . .

Inveterate elegist,
he mulls the hours
—his smashed cargo like
marble statues gleaming

through cloudy silt, weeds,
his ghosts, degraded
as bottom-feeders,
boring like worms

in his mind's split grain:
Thrashing inside him
who is this other more
constant than Penelope—?

this self-conniver
who destroys the crew
while he who set
the course goes free . . .

He eyes the mop
like a twin brother,
its soapy, snaky,
steaming head swooping

down across the tiles
to devour reflected stars
until the night
is shadowless, motionless . . .

But the night is never
shadowless, never motionless—
his eyes bleed into
salty mist weaving,

unweaving above the foam
like a shuttle passing
through invisible threads
his hand can't snip from the frame:

Fitful in his sleep, his bed
like stone, he turns
and twists in
tangling weedy arms,

the wreck reaching up
to drag him down
while the monster
chuckling and choking

in his dream
waits for daylight
to carry him back home:
Its eyes are wet.

Achilles' Horses

Achilles' horses are weeping,
                    for dead Patroclus weeping,
While the son of Cronus temporizes,
                    "Why were you given to Peleus,
Why should you learn that men are miserable,
                    you who were born immortal?"

But the horses weep such tears,
                    they weep such heavy tears
That they stand like marble
                    on the edge of the field of battle,
Their sorrow sharper
                    than the whip of the charioteer,
Their sorrow more bitter
                    than the earth can bear

—Frozen like the horses I saw carved from ice
                    standing in a field at dusk,
Their manes and haunches and scored faces
                    lit by our headlights' scouring fierceness
So that they leaped against the darkness,
                    rearing and kicking against
The high-beams like swords slashing . . .

The horses, steered by the gods back to the fighting,
Feel the goad of Achilles' fury—
                    "Bring me back alive—don't leave me to die
The way you did Patroclus—"
                    feel it rising like a fume as Xanthus
Slips his yoke and senses human words rising,
                    rising in his throat, guiding
His tongue to prophesy:
                    "We will bring you back to safety
This time Achilles—
                    but know that your death is
Nearer with each step we take . . ."
                    Ready now to bear the yoke,
The horse, shaking off a fly,
                    turns his head away.

The Fight

*And they shall go forth, and look upon the carcasses of men that have
transgressed against me . . .*

—Isaiah, 66:24

The street speaks the language of the street
—*Dumb ass Jesus freak! Who you think you are?*
until he goes berserk, shining-eyed preacher,

his straight razor in his pale fist making them scatter.
Face anointed with tears he can't blink back,
he stands alone in the intersection;

a car begins to honk, another and another,
and soon everyone is honking
until the Lord's chosen, abandoned, proud,

wanders to the sidewalk and leans against a lamppost
—so inwound into himself he doesn't notice us,
bystanders who gawk or look away,

his passion unfathomed as the madness
falling upon Saul, Saul who hurls
his javelin at David whom he loves:

he seems both together, Saul's madness
and David's slender strength, his rage
and frailty volatile in the air, his razor

shaky in his hand. He moves off through
shimmering exhaust as they dodge and mock,
his smooth, hairless face spectral in the fumes

I penetrate, imagining his heartbeat
racing in my ears: What do I know of him
but his clothes and skin, the text he sob-shouts,

The broad walls of Babylon shall be utterly broken . . . ?
I try to hold him in mind, to see him reading
at his Bible in the quiet of dawn, pronouncing

the words to himself as he sits in a chair
or lies on a bed, the lamp beside him
casting its light across the well-thumbed page,

scholar of his book, lover of the Word,
his Bible holding demons and gods and the God
of his desire, of his rage, pain distilled

into His love, the cover worn smooth by
reverential hands . . . but the sidewalk
bears him off, tugging him from me,

his fate covert, private, all his own,
fending off my gaze reluctant to let him go;
his fury and tears choking up the words

he hurls at his tormentors—*Bastards, lousy*
bastards, just steer clear of me, OK?
just steer the fuck clear—still dodging, mocking . . .

I keep my distance from his razor and his tormentors,
too scared to intervene, my boundaries drawn
as if I looked down on him from Heaven

the way the saved look down at the damned,
my eyes riveted by his abandonment and pain . . . and yes,
mingling with my sorrow and compassion—

my heart unveiled to His all-seeing eye
whose Dark as well as Light refracts through every soul—
a mute satisfaction pulsing in my veins.

The Harbor

1. Mosaic

Your face clears of expression, your eyes
Turn inward even as your gaze
Searches mine—
        and then the sixth sense,
Like being blinded by floodlights, the audience
Blacked out, that we're playing different scenes,
Your voice prompting as I stumble through my lines—
"Richer and for poorer" "sickness and in health" "till death"—
And see, as you look at me, myself
Like ocean fog, my limits rolling
Back on waters stretching smooth, then churning
White and black in last night's dream
Weirdly neutral, spectral, but foreknown,
You and I changed to mermaid, merman
—Diving together through waves of rippling stone
That gleam and run in the heat-scarfed sun,
Our flesh/fish bodies puddling molten.

2. Bath

Buoyancy lifting us on each wave's crest,
Probing eye peering from the deep, is it you
Rising, scales undulant, steaming,
Breath heaving in the calm, nostrils quavering?

Our sweat pungent as a love potion, we watch
Light zigzag down the tiles to scan
Across our bodies as you take us down
—We drown in you, you vomit us up,

And still you can't keep off, your wake's
Backwash swirling headlong into your mouth
As you whirlpool round us toiling through
The swell of your razoring whiplash tail.

3. Argument

The lighthouse light there, then not,
The wide-planked blue floor mirrored out
The window in the wave-run
Breaking on shore. The house still

But for a faraway plane's engine
Cutting out. Suspension in pure ether
Of four o'clock dark . . . The soul-oval
Of lamplight on the desk grows tense

With an out-of-season gnat's nervous
Coptering: In the motion
Of those tiny wings I conjure
Your bracing dart and thrust

Scattering the freak of starlight
Pulsing on the pane, the whole house
Cocked, inwound as an ear:
Furnace-roar echoes through joists

And floorboards and a hammering
Quickens that can't be stopped, doubling,
Redoubling, the nail-blows echoing
Higher and higher up the scale.

4. Harpoon

The wooden handle cracked but seasoned tough,
The harpoon looked to have been waiting for us,
To have pushed through its own corona of rust
The way light pushes through a cloud.

Junk-store denizen, it stood on guard,
Veteran, persevering, wary for the next round
Though bypassed, out of bounds—the length
Of barbed steel just the distance eye to eye

You took toward me when one night on the roof
We smelled diesel from the harbor,
Pure stench of oil and brine, acrid, spoiling
Like blood-warm flesh—but longed for

Once it's gone . . . Steel head glinting
In the shifting light, it stands alert in the house,
Not a blessing or a curse, but potential
Thrumming through it to outdo

The aiming hand and fly into a future
Where its sheen like fishscales skimming
Above dark water leaves a trail
Phosphorescing, daring us on—but only

Per usual, day to day, the way saltwater,
Vanishing overnight, crusts into
Light-angled pillars and spires, slight
Crystal on crystal holding fast.

The Door

Fifteen years in each other's heat
And you still picture me the single man
Living hand-to-mouth on my own heart . . .

And you, how do I see you? The question
Stinging, my eyes slide off yours,
Your poker-faced stare become another barrier—

It's as if who we thought we'd be to one another
Waits outside knocking on the door,
At first composed, then pounding so hard

The door no longer is an entrance in
But the one thing we must always keep closed.
And so we wonder what that face

Beyond the door looks like until it rears
Like mist in the steaming sun, that stranger's
Always shifting, spotlit glance egging us onward

To the verge of space where we sense love
As we've never known unstoppably expanding,
Billowing and towering through the clear deep noon . . .

—And yet those features burn off
In the heat and leave us still facing
The warped-shut door and what we know is true:

The sun shining impartially back into our eyes
With a light that we both love and half-despise;
Your face as it appears to me; mine as it seems to you.

IV

To the Sun

Crowned in hydrogen, it travels incognito,
visiting equally the mansions on Brattle
as the mad and dying in City Hospital,
its warmth bereaving for being impersonal.

Friend to all that dies in spite of its spring heat,
it ghosts across windows of highrises half-built
and brick-faced warehouses
reflected in the river, it makes

the trash trees in alleyways glitter,
acid green stinging as the day clearing of rain . . .
Come to my friend's mother painfully swallowing
raging, aphasic, who pushes away her food,

allows herself and her daughter not one word.
Come like the volunteer that strokes
her cheek until her body heat
diffuses, her blood starts to cool . . .

X-ray eye penetrating to our souls,
show us to ourselves as we bullshit and scheme,
help us to survive our own stung minds
swarming day and night with cock/cunt dreams . . .

Come as a conqueror whose molten heat
makes sunbathers and street people sack out,
their mouths yawning open to demons
who slip in and out of us whatever our lives,

shed your light on trash cans sprawling in the street,
stir the vacant lots to rank weeds tangling, pushing
through asphalt as no matter what the soil
you guide us toward your heat,

oh blinding father, enemy of blight
who drives us to the shade, give us this hour
to hang by the river and pass around the wine
until our minds buzz like hives of honeyed light.

One Sunday

Something in the mind can't rest, can it,
the mind is like that, my mind, yours, scavenging

after objects it gnaws, spits out, infantile
explorer day and night . . . Take one Sunday,

the bells clashing in the treetops as I cross
The Common, my Walkman trilling flute notes

—blackout in my head: it's Agincourt
unreeling in the Roxy thirty years ago, England's

arrows jumpcut to French knights charging
while my eyes parry bludgeons, swords thrusting,

horses toppling onto knights cursing, screaming—
then my mind rewound to Olivier cloaked

as a commoner, sounding his troops' mettle
the night before battle while the boy soldier muses:

When all those legs and arms and heads chopped off
shall join together at the latter day,

if the King and his cause be not just, he hath
a heavy reckoning . . . Flute notes like arrows

showering down dissolved to tape hiss as
I took off the headphones, sun flicking on

like houselights glazing the Sheraton Commander's
awning of gay bunting beneath which loitered

unattended a nomad shopping cart, its smell
of old tomatoes pungent and sweet:

she emerged from the hedge as if from the wings,
her gestures broad and slow like someone acting—

but not acting, too, not, in her difference,
Olivier in makeup making himself other

as she offered in a stage whisper someone or something
invisible a candy bar, flirting with it, confiding, laughing

with this alien stranger spellbound in our world
whose spectral charm enchants her, talking fondly

on and on in an indecipherable slur
—though now she was cooing as to an infant

or animal, her fingers stroking, caressing,
maternally hectoring, as whoever or whatever

leaned into her hand, its head like a unicorn's
nuzzling with such rapture it couldn't get enough,

nothing in this world could be enough—
at other times in the park I've seen her asleep

or sparechanging with an air of holiday leisure,
nodding at you, her eyes friendly whether you give or not,

her youth still present in her face and gestures . . .
But that Sunday she was different,

another part of her mind pushing that other self aside:
I watch her draw back, her arm stretching forth

as if her hand held a sword to which she
forces it to kneel, head bowed to work her will

while she mouths curses, regal before her thrall:
serving man, assassin, demon lover, fool?—

her swordpoint at its throat uttering
oaths that she exacts this Sunday morning,

October 6, 1996, between
The Common and the Sheraton Commander.

The Train

Train wheels like battle sounds lulled the carriage
While the train ran down the track the way
The charging blues and grays, colliding, collided

With death that we controlled with dice rolling
Charge, Retreat. The sun darkened, across the plain
Night advanced, the blue giving ground to the gray

Sweeping forward, the joy of boys playing
Their boardgame hour after hour deepening
To such intent pleasure that the train itself

Seemed to disappear—from the aisle-light flickering down
Our seat came unmoored as if it were an island
Moving on a dark ocean and trailing long roots

Like anchor chains dragging through depths
Where I heard voices murmuring
About the hellish cold and equally hellish heat,

About stops on the schedule that the engine,
Devouring mile on mile of silver rail,
Sped through as if racing toward oblivion.

Through musket smoke billowing the soldiers
Called out their eternal death shouts, those voices
From the depths that wound through their battle cries

Inextricable, not to be denied
In the thrust, tussle, deep satisfaction
Of falling freefall into deathless battle

Against the foe while the train in its rapture
Moved unceasingly over the invisible rails.
The compartment was black now, and the dead troops,

Invincibly dead, roved under the earth
The way water roves under an island
Drifting rootless all night above the deep.

Flesh

He is still flesh, animal flesh whatever worlds his madness
moves him back and forth between, the world of living names
that he speed-raps with a delirious, driven virtuosity
". . . SchmitSmithSmitheSmithers . . ." and the world of the divine
in which the Unnamed lodges at the center of his brain
giving orders, routing through his neurons the universal wires

whose masterful control of all things—the cancer that he wills
to flourish or wither, the war that ends because his thought-waves
signal the Powers to possess the hearts of presidents
and their chart-explicating generals—now battles his flesh, flesh sweating,
flesh so tensed that trying to get him to lie down
is to sense inside his body a malicious energy turning back

on itself and so enraged at having been contained
it beats back all the fiercer my calming words and gestures,
impossible to assuage as it strives to escape
his body that, still sanely cautious, holds him back
from the windows and makes him skirt the doorway,
spooked by what will happen if he steps out of the room,

his laughter edgy with the fearful elation
of that power that elects his flesh to this suffering
it stages before me as he doggedly keeps circling,
reciting always faster name after name, this force
contriving to pull his body ever farther into
its shimmering field of power so that he begins

to tremble the way a horse once trembled
when I rode into barbed wire invisible beneath high weeds
and kept spurring forward until I climbed down
and brushed against the wounds, blood soaking
through my shirt to wet my skin, just as this power
now pouring from his skin seems to flood

into the void his gibbering hollows inside my brain
swelling with that syllable atrocious and banal
as he trembles and sweats and then begins
to scribble the forbidden Name of the Unnamed
so that the letters loop and lunge like flames
while his hand shakes and shakes holding the pencil.

Transfusion

I saw it, visible aura, unstoppable flow—
the stream pouring down the walls in waters
everlasting that the damned below

reach out their arms to with such longing—
men, women, their small round bellies attractive
in that light, even to the demons tormenting

them with pitchforks, voluptuous
moments of degradation . . .
Suffering souls, what do you ask of us

looking up in wonder at the golden deer
in the mosaic dome, its muzzle nuzzling
the stream's ruby drops, its eyes' cool glimmer

gazing unconcerned . . . ? Ghostly loins flicker
in woozy candlelight, the stained glass
grimy as linoleum lozenges under

the patients' feet in the hospital
across the street, legs unsteady beneath
their johnnies as they stagger down the hall

like models on a runway showing off cancer,
stroke, immune systems gone haywire,
the blood-starved brain straining to remember:

Burning in their eyes gleam the drops
everlasting that the nurse's hand controls,
screwing down the valve that slows the drops

to a drowsy crawl, the needles aching
in their arms leading back up the tubes
to the blood bags burning . . . reminding

me of when my own face, pale, too pale, turned
like a flower to that draining sun
hazy through storming clouds of neon . . . :

As I drifted beyond my body
in a fever dream, I saw a stag, white-furred,
its eyes staring into mine until I

felt suspended in those pupils' dead-level:
Swirling round its hoof the stream
pulsed in the twilight; its muzzle

lowered to drink as that shimmering
dissolved me and cascaded over boulders, the streambed
leading to the treeline: Like steam hissing,

somnambulant as lava, my own dead gathered,
faces sprouting fur, infirmities thrown off
in paws and hooves, everything they'd suffered

forgotten . . . but as I moved among their claws
and fangs, calling out their names, no trace of
who they'd been glistened in their eyes

gone vacant as the dark rearing up in the vaulted nave . . .
Now the golden deer gazes at the tree
of faces that sprouts from Jesse's thighs,

its sap rising through the stem to flower in
the man-god, the leaded panes that shape
his head and body seeming almost molten—

as if he'd just taken form from a pool
of magma, his face tinged red as a single corpuscle
rushing headlong, fraught with potential—until

the sun kindles his face to bloody streams
pouring down the walls in which the damned
now seem to bathe: Their pale limbs

flush, veins pulse, aroused bodies hungering
to touch our hands, our faces, and be touched—
breasts, bellies, encircling arms, pure flesh dazzling

even the demons' twisted faces
penetrated by those imploring eyes,
all of us afloat in the ocean of their gazes

—the damned in this light no longer damned,
their bodies only bodies, like ours
soft, round . . . The light shifts, the damned

dwindle among the demons, their eyes flattening
into pain . . . Now, only the deer's eyes
pierce the flooding dark, the pupils staring

through us turning us to stone . . . until we turn
away abashed before that gaze, as if
the soul shed its mask to stare its keeper down.

The Wreck

Spirit, is it, or only my own mind
miming spirit, my eyes its eyes
as it looks down on me from on top

of the city, seeing me stalled in traffic
at the wreck, willing my mind to wander
from the driver strapped to his stretcher

to the stoplight where the brownstone
feeds its corners into the mist. Penetrated
by that gaze I seem to recognize,

can it be your spirit, my friend,
dead these twenty years, still unsatisfied
with all the dead *don't* know—the how and why

of being dead each moment? The land
of the dead unknowable as your gaze
that baffles me with whether it's really yours?

Or only some reflex I sense firing,
relaxing, when I swerve through traffic
in the January dusk? . . . the momentum

of each car behind its headlights slowing
to a halt at this scorched hulk
in the ditch. Do you long through me

to again pump the accelerator, press the brake,
body spinning one way, mind another, caught
in traffic's omniscient crossfire?

Or is this only the hangover of last night's
nightmare, the car infinitely gliding into
the oncoming lane that drops off

into a gulf, blank pupil of a slick
too wide to jump, too deep to cross?
Or maybe we *are* one, my eyes your eyes

confronting me in headlights from the oncoming lane,
the speeding faces zooming past like film frames
of the injured driver's face, each eye

an *x* of darkness, his mouth crimped around
its primal "yes" "no." Now you peer down at the stretcher,
the driver's face gone white, expressionlessly calm,

his pain like blood pulsing in numb hands—*your* hands
reaching out through his
to the wreck's wheel until in your wonder you forget

that flesh would only weigh you down
as you hover in its flames trying
to get warm . . . But that fire's gone out, traffic still stalled,

my car's heater barely warming
my fingers as I stare
at the shattered railing his car

crashed through, the odometer stalled on
a number the driver never saw . . . The cracked
windshield like a transparent skull

flickers in the scattered flares,
the absence in the empty driver's seat
staring at the frozen numerals

watching for them to come back round to zeroes.

A Visit

What she is waiting for never arrives
or arrives so slowly she can't see it:
    Like the river
    bluing silver

and wearing minutely deeper into its channel,
the flow hardens to carved stone as she fidgets
    beneath the whirling fan
    impatient for the train

that rocks us above the water to arrive:
Her sisters and brothers gone, she ventures alone
    through sunlight
    and moonlight

weaving shadowy faces across the peeling walls . . .
—Speeding toward her, is it you and me she spies
    in the trembling train
    windows while the engine

hauls us down rails that swerve under wheels
rolling through her brain? Faces burn
    through dirty glass,
    smears of lips and eyes

dissolve to spots of darkness swarming between
her eyes so that swaying apartment towers
      crumble as her nostrils
      prickle from the landfill's

ammonia that hangs above the stacked, crushed cars.
The rails that take us to her pass boxcar after boxcar
      like the successive selves we are
      as she dreams us coming closer,

switching track to track: Now the super unbolts
her door as she calls: "Oh is it really you?"
      —the wheels rolling
      through her head bringing

us face to face with raveled bandages, crutches
leaned in dusty corners, terraced mountains of
      yellowing newspaper.
      Framed above her chair

a picture of a prairie sprawls round a covered wagon
and the horse she rode as a girl, her eyes
      fading points of light . . .
      Again she calls out

above the train's approaching rumble: "Is it you at last?
My eyes have got so bad peoples' faces
      are all blurry . . . Now
      tell me, is it *really* you?"

But already the rails are switching, bearing
our waving hands away at the speed of thought
      over the stony waters that
      ceaselessly pour out.

The Grid

Faces swell, then flatten into the million-celled grid
of windows that keeps replicating day and night
until no part of the sky remains unlit.

Words spoken between chasms of the avenues
are sucked up into stillness after rain:
Is my strength the strength of stones? Is my flesh of brass?

Lying on the sidewalk, tendons bulging in his wrists,
he stares straight into the armada of rush hour shoes,
his head lolling backward at a hard right angle to his neck

as the police hoist him by his armpits and sockless ankles.
Under the purple blackness of his face
a jaundiced pallor shadows the whites, unblinking, of his eyes.

The waters wear the stones. My face is foul with weeping
and on my eyelids is the shadow of death.
Sunlight steams up from humid pavement,

the subway air-shafts warmly breathe,
the parapets of the bridge towers gleam
through mist swirling off the water's satin-sheen.

Smoking, joking, he used to recline on one elbow
in front of the storefronts' steel-grated doors,
his boutique laid out on the sidewalk: A child's overalls,

soggy magazines, jewelry nicked and scratched . . .
Down river, huddled on thin ledges of granite
the fledging kestrels reach toward their mothers' beaks,

the traffic blare funneling up past the office windows
to expand and mingle with the brine-tinged air,
the tugboats lifting and falling in the swell

that rolls beneath the heaving pier. Now another vendor
spreads out his wares in the same square of sidewalk, his hands
gently laying out each cast-off garment.

The other's goods still lie on the cement-damp
canvas laundry sack that each day he carefully unpacked.
By midnight his sack will be scavenged clean,

the aura of his hands on the canvas
already fading beneath the warmth of another's palms,
his square of the city washing back into the grid

that arranges and rearranges into the lights and darks
of numbered faces pressed into the coroner's files . . .
Hast thou entered into the springs of the sea?

Have the gates of death been opened unto thee?
When I looked for good, then evil came unto me.
The river's mouth widens, pouring out past

the harbor to open ocean, black swells
running off the freighters' hulls. Drifting in the mist
looms the island where they hung the mutineer,

up river lies the entrance to the tunnel
that runs beneath the waters,
those cuttings mark the tracks that radiate outward

toward the cities spread out across the plain,
and there under the mountain through lightless caverns
the sun at night makes its smoldering way.

Purity Supreme

Space station walls
              of my bedroom revolving
as in my head
              the floodlit aisles
throb, blankly ecstatic, the figures in the aisles

of store cop, stockboy,
              of man in dark suit
and burgundy fedora
              they push
to the storeback, voices intertwining *Go on*

I done nothing get out
              don't mess with me—their figures
spiral out, constellations
              wheeling insensibly
as in each face, under stretched taut skin,

the night's emblems burn
              incarnate in them—
but then too personal for that,
              their features meld
to the face of a man waiting in the checkout line

whose knees
              keep jerking on their own
as if always he was
              climbing stairs up
and up, resting on one landing,

his face coolly nonchalant,
              then twitching, twitching,
when, beyond his control
              another staircase lowers
from the air that his knees thinking on their own

climb and climb,
              his head tilting back
as if scanning for the top
              but the top keeps receding,
his feet keep lifting, shuffling, as midnight strikes

and passes over
              as in the back they wrestle
to the floor and handcuff
              the man shouting *Don't mess with me*—
the stars revolving in ever spreading black the man

climbing the stairs
              climbs up through ceaselessly
while below tiers of windows jitter
              in Central Square deserted to dark rain
falling with one long murmur of conspiring laughter.

Raft

Dr. Pepper and the Bible on the shelf together, a tricycle
                  laying tracks through
the rare snow of a Texas winter, a new green Plymouth Valiant
with fins and a V-6, a drive-in theater screen, blacks to the left,
                  whites right,
       ripples on water like the damned being
               winnowed from the saved;
          oh black-browed history, on your raft
we float, your raft cobbled from dead languages, bones, fires,
      dust-hung fields sprouting pylons, towers, domes,
from rivering taxis, radio waves, wide pre-reflecting eyes channeling
            through the city's circuit-woven brain
enwound with subway vaults and girdered catacombs
              while Lethe's waters open
                to swallow
         us, languorous, taking their time . . .
As boys, my brothers and I found logs strapped with fraying rope
      and drifting on a pond, Tony's Grove—
             the mountains fell
         sheer into still water that trapped
feathers, leaves, berries, bark, fishbones, beaver bones,
the heaviness of water dragging it all down:

Sharp-eyed presence,
buoy us up on this raft once made of logs but now
only of words, from traces
of woodsmoke and frying pan, from saplings chewed by beaver
and beaver stuffed
and staring back from dim vitrines, from huts and treasure hoards
hidden in
back alleys of apartment buildings crumbling
the way aqueducts, temples, menhirs, dolmens crumbled
and were scavenged
for cornerstones to celebrate new gods and ward off
demons and mad souls
trapped in trees, from TV warriors noble as the Roman
Marius and barbarian Jugurtha, from Cassius Clay
who rose up
Muhammad Ali once Liston from
the Lewiston Penitentiary went down, taciturn Liston moving
stolid in the ring, from dynasties of *Yankees*
Ford, Mantle, Maris,
from *Giant* Mays of the basket catch
and Willie McCovey the slugger and the high-kicking windup
of fastballer Marichal
while the basement bombshelter in hushed silence attends
devotions of
canned goods gleaming on steel shelves,
from wires crisscrossing, sparking, fusing in the overloaded brain,
oh gone and battered traces all lashed together with intricate knots
memory now fumbles to untie:

Again we step
onto the raft riding low under our weight, the logs' gaps
        letting water seep through that rots the rope
even as we splash one another, wrestle, dive . . . sit drifting on
the raft, a chill on the ripples as sun feathers
        behind a peak and the pond
reflects our faces peering over the raft's edge, our faces
            so calm—
        faces of brothers
unconscious of past or future, who lie on a raft
        in cool negligence of each other's presence,
adrift, absorbed, our swimming suits drying, then dried.

The Ticket

False-faced monument, monument of mind that fades
into the story a friend tells in a bar—how her mother
and father survived Dachau together, then made each other
unhappy for thirty years . . . though in the camp her mother
seemed to flourish, nicknamed "the Angel" for helping
the sick, the old . . . but after the War grew negligent,
despondent, as if ordinary life was life among
the dead, the Angel haunting as she cooked, cleaned,
her own face reproaching her for having filled in,
the Angel's hollow cheekbones still sharp under her skin:

Monument of brick, of crumbling mortar, of a chimney
toppling broken-backed: Sign that reads "Ten thousand by day,
ten thousand by night"—the eye prying at the neat stone houses
in the town tight-shut, repulsed by the sentry box
at the nearby Army base, one-way glass impenetrably smoked.
Bulb flash; snapshot—I watch a father pose his wife and kids
under the entry gate as around us the camp staggers in the heat . . .
Faces flattened into photographs dissolve into dots swarming against
the eye that pushes to see through them to the living face behind
but the face keeps submerging into that blurring wash:

Monument estranging because its image lasts, monument less real
because the eye can see it whole; lassitude of spirit, horror learned
by rote, stagy strangeness of the preserved gas chamber (it smells
of clay, rank sweetly moldering clay): The Angel now a wrinkled
smoke-dark woman who warily half-smiles in a wallet photograph,
her eyes holding my eyes off, her image defiled by my looking past
the image, wanting more and more; that hunger devolving into
film-eyed suffering, smoke of prehistory smearing over history:
Grease of millennial ash that blackens a stone roof, cannon bones
whitening heaped among cattle skulls, toothless ransacked jaws:

Monument untranslatable, monument that runs parallel
to the Neanderthal family flickering huge across the screen, the child
I was agog at *Tyrannosaurus rex* stalking them, mechanical:
The ticket in my hand that gives entry to these shades,
moment of spectral smoke skeining from a cigarette,
voices still thirsting to tell what they lived and died,
voices asking our protection in the drifting shifts
and lapses of our attention, the Angel still haunting,
a self-haunter: Monument of mouth turned down at us,
mouth moving: Once you were the Angel; now what are you?

Speech for Myself as a Ghost

"Whoever I was, whatever I may have done, speaks to me
and you now in the voice of this rainy light carrying us back
to where moments ago I *was* the steam rising from your coffee

and then further back to a room made shadowy by sunlight,
a Murphy bed covered by red curtains, and bottle brush blooms
that hummingbirds needle with such appetite;

and then to a wheelchair where your father sits and stares
not knowing that we're there, and back further to when
hot milk scalds my tongue, an air raid siren blares,

mosquitoes buzz grainy as newsreel bombs
that fall in clusters in the drive-in's dark, the projector's beam
wavering through those bloodsipping swarms

—and back to where the door the dead enter so freely
it's as if they hadn't died opens to orchard rows
of cherry trees whitening the air as crows, flocking, fly

branch to branch, a stick beats time to *caw caw   caw caw,*
an irrigation ditch fills while the promised land
brims over its reflection until it swamps the window

so that now we hear what throbs in each marrow bone:
a phantom heartbeat that, slowly counting down,
echoes in the iced-over sectors of the brain

where ghosts crowding to hear that fading pulse
meld with one another mist into mist
and melt back into the wash of uncreated Chaos

(. . . that place in which nothing gestures to nothing else,
least of all this voice straining to reach you widowed
by these words that suddenly ring false)

—your coffee gone lukewarm as under dormant boughs
a trash fire ignites a drop of rain
coolly transparent through migrant shadows."

The Field

Once I left the room
of the boardinghouse
I dreamed, I saw at the end
of a long fallow field

the derricks and cranes
like spider-woven filament
against the bay
curdling in the sun.

The clods of earth
beneath my shoes
crumbled at each step
and reeked of ammonia,

that friable breaking up
like a quavering voice
leaping to attack,
laddering up and down

a dissonant scale
so pure, so atonal
that it shivered all through me
as if I were a tuning fork

vibrating through
the far-echoing afternoon.
On and on my feet
kept moving, the softly

combusting clods
cushioning each step
as before me the field spread
always larger and more still,

the dream taking me
wherever I would go,
my black shadow
plunging and lifting

like a plough—
until I was borne up
by the buoyant exhaustion
of my path down

the furrows that flowed out
like a never-ending note
floating on the breath
of a singer whose eyes shut

and who feels himself lifted
past the spotlit hall
into a solitude beyond
appeal or recall.